# MONSTER
## ROAD BUILDERS

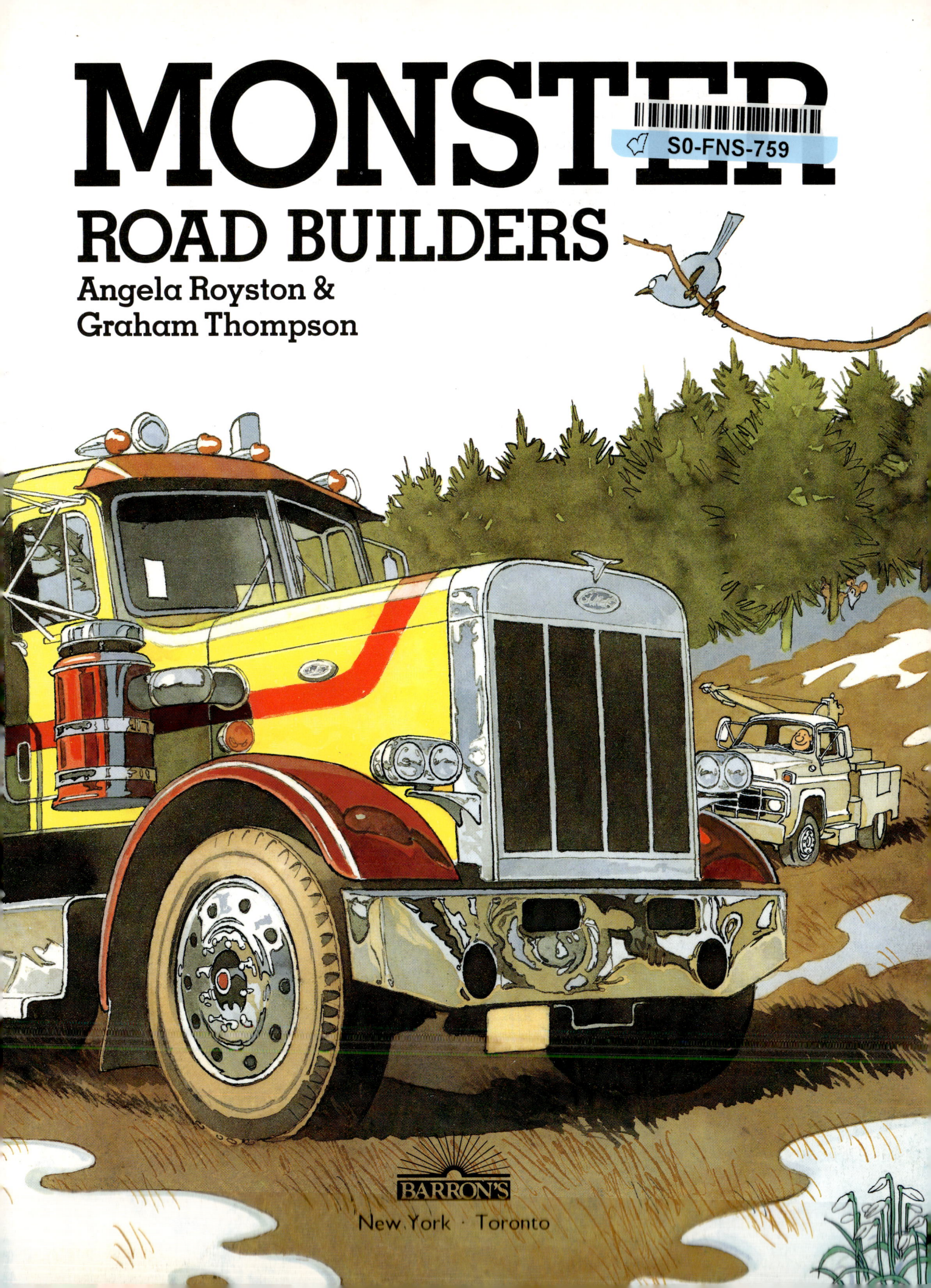

Angela Royston &
Graham Thompson

BARRON'S
New York · Toronto

# Bulldozer

Monster machines have come to build a new road.
This powerful bulldozer is pushing aside rocks and earth. Trees and bushes come crashing down.

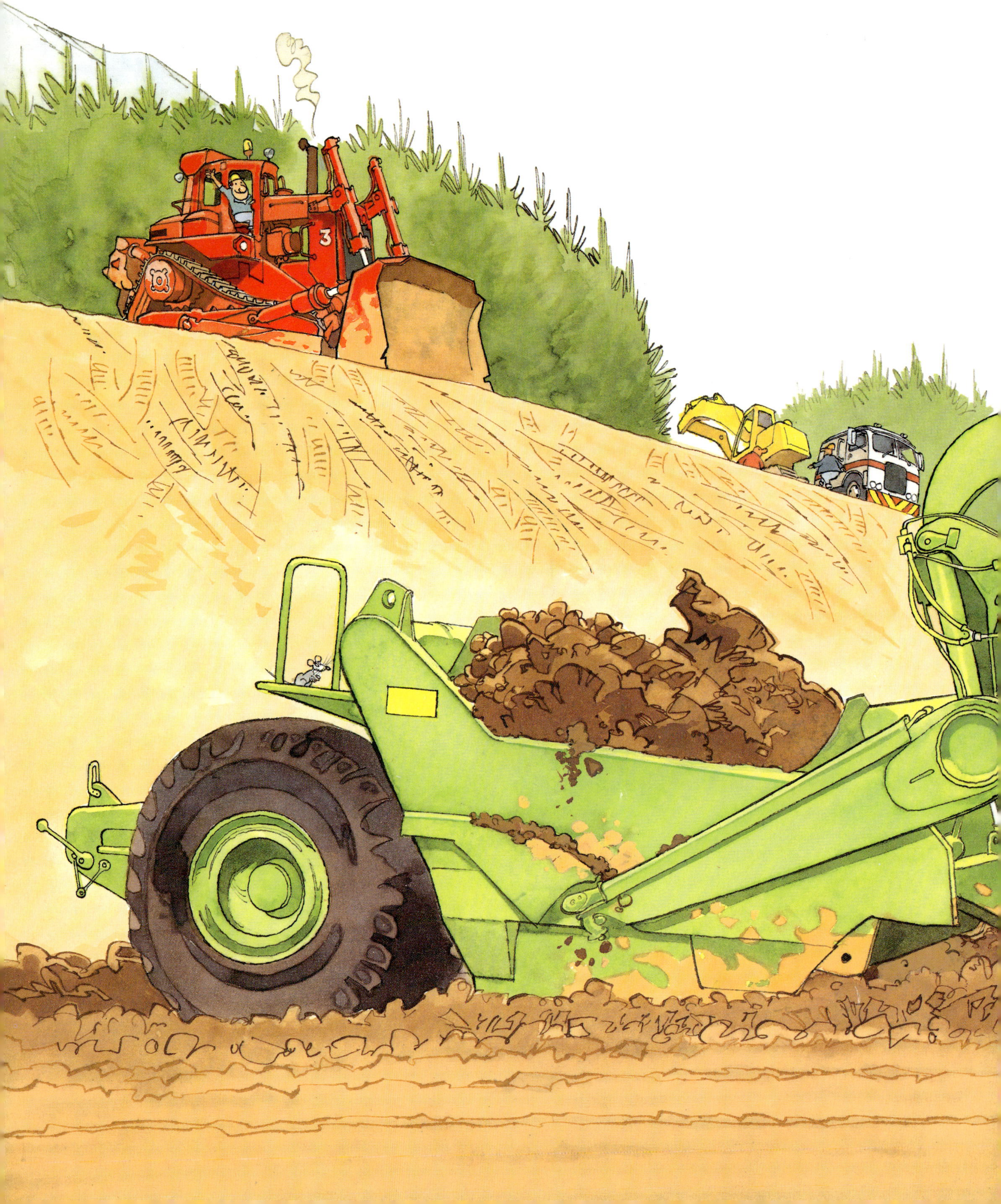
3

# Scraper

The scraper is clearing the ground. Its big blade slices the earth and pushes it into the huge bin.
Here comes the bulldozer to help the scraper along.

# Excavator

These excavators are loading earth into a dump truck.
The enormous bucket reaches out and scoops up some earth. Then the huge arm lifts and swings the bucket over to the dump truck. The bucket tips and the earth drops into the truck.

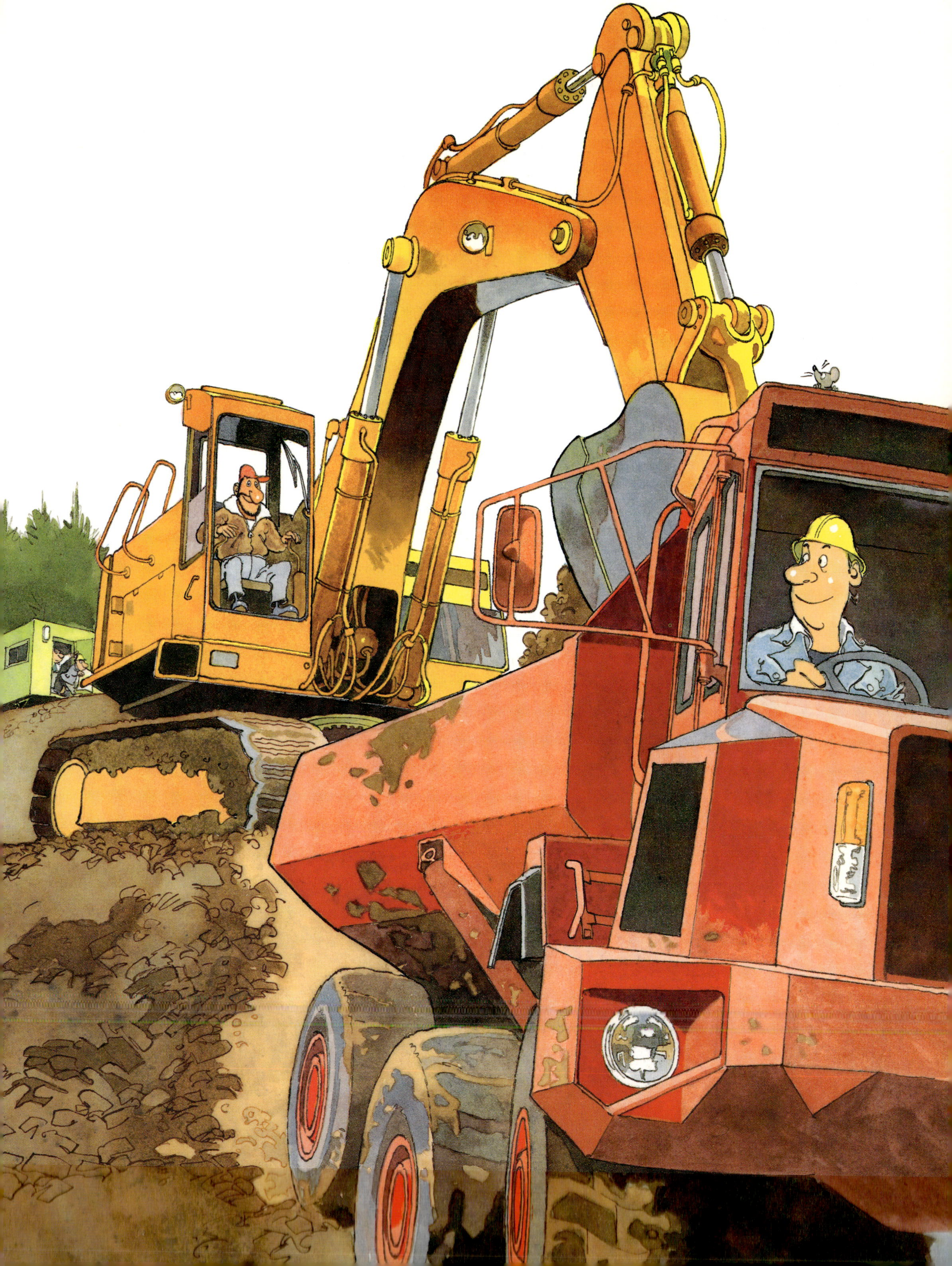

# Dump Truck

The dump truck takes the earth to fill in a hole in the road.
The back tilts up and the earth tumbles out.

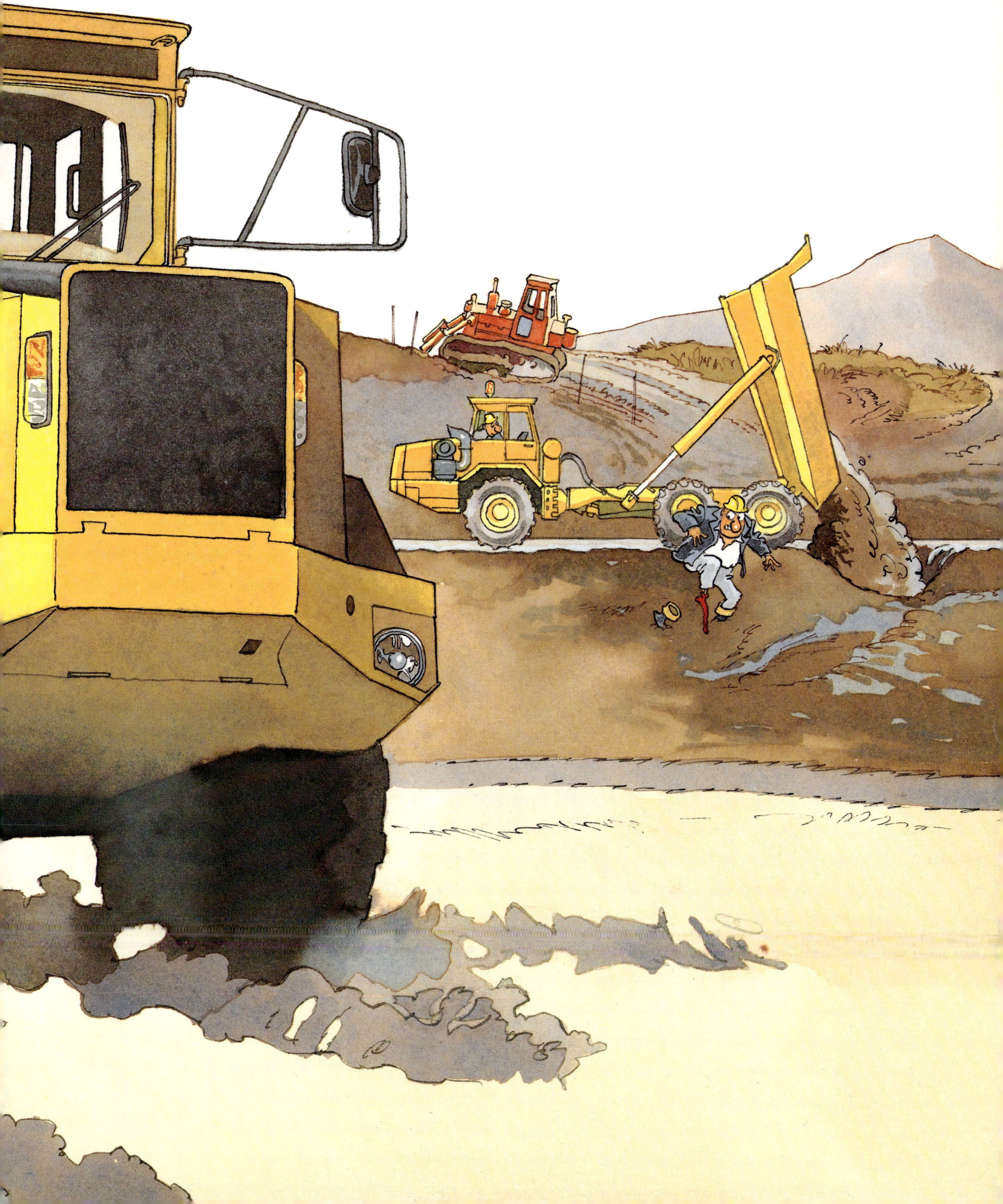

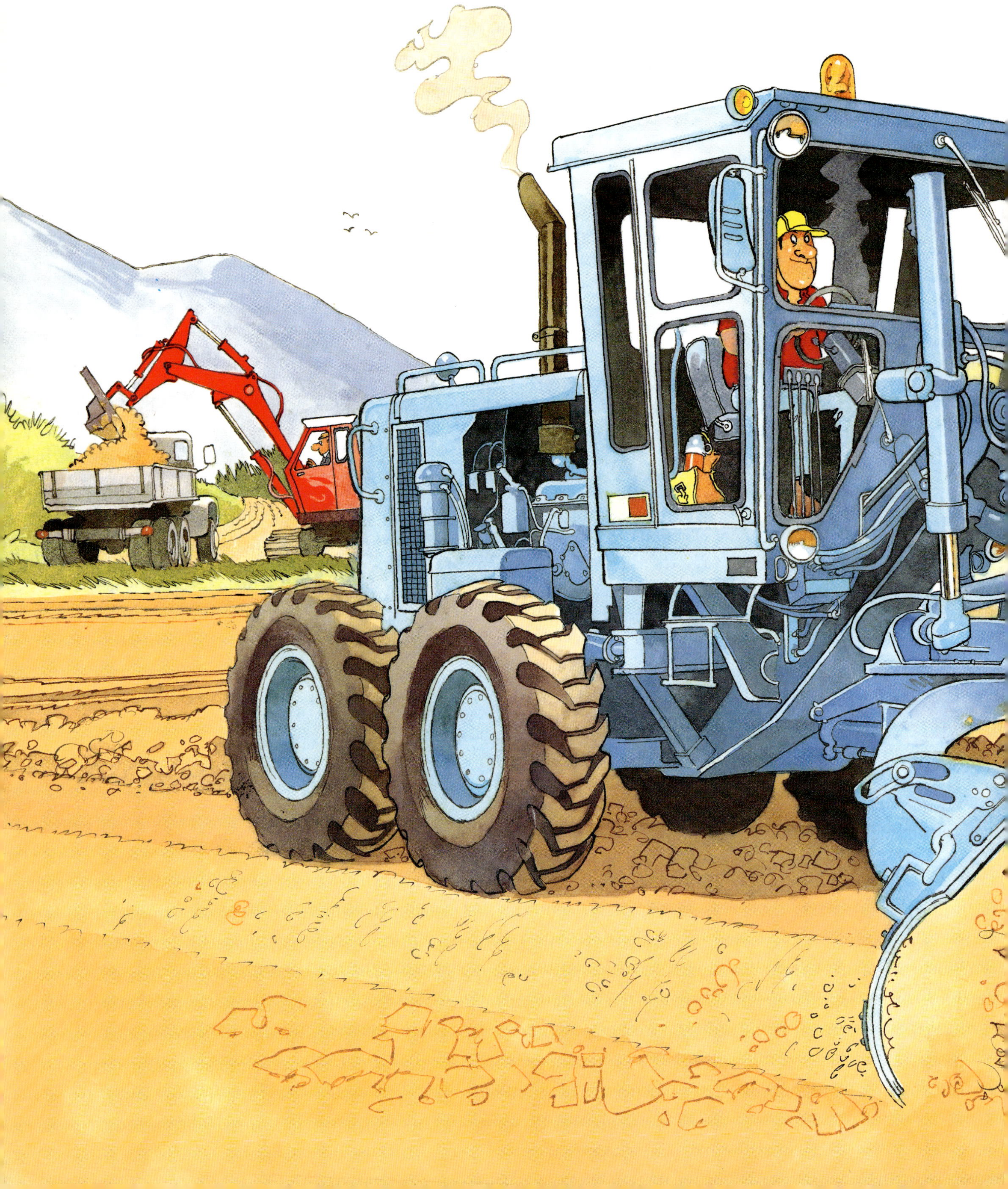

# Grader

This grader makes the road smooth. Its heavy blue blade scrapes away bumps and fills in holes.
The blade is tilted so the road will slope down at the sides and rain will run off it.

# Backhoe

This backhoe is digging a drain beside the road for rainwater to pour into. The bucket and boom dig up the soil like a huge metal hand and arm.

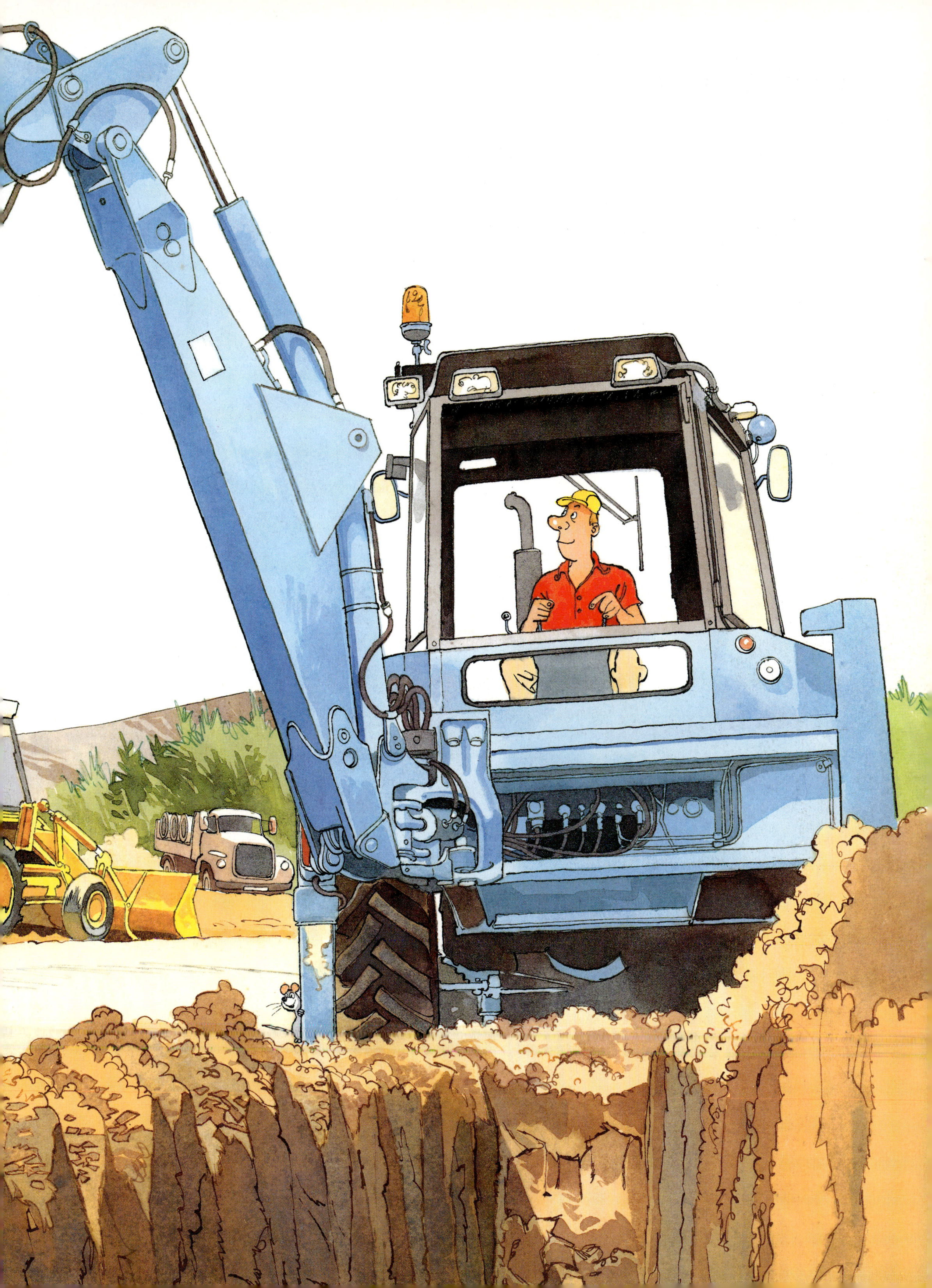

# Paver

Now the road is ready to be tarred. The hot sticky asphalt slides slowly out of the dump truck into the paver. The paver spreads it over the road.

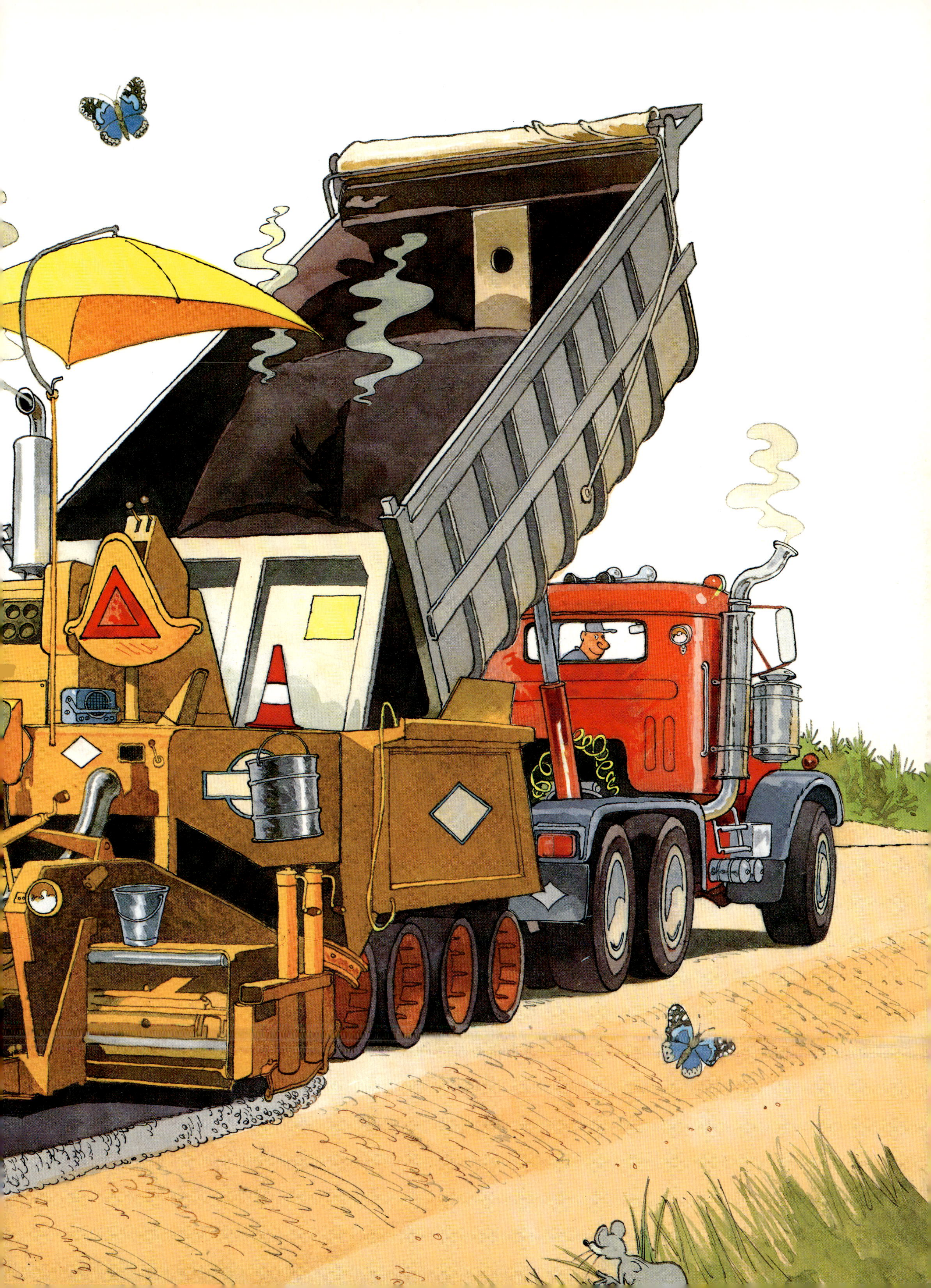

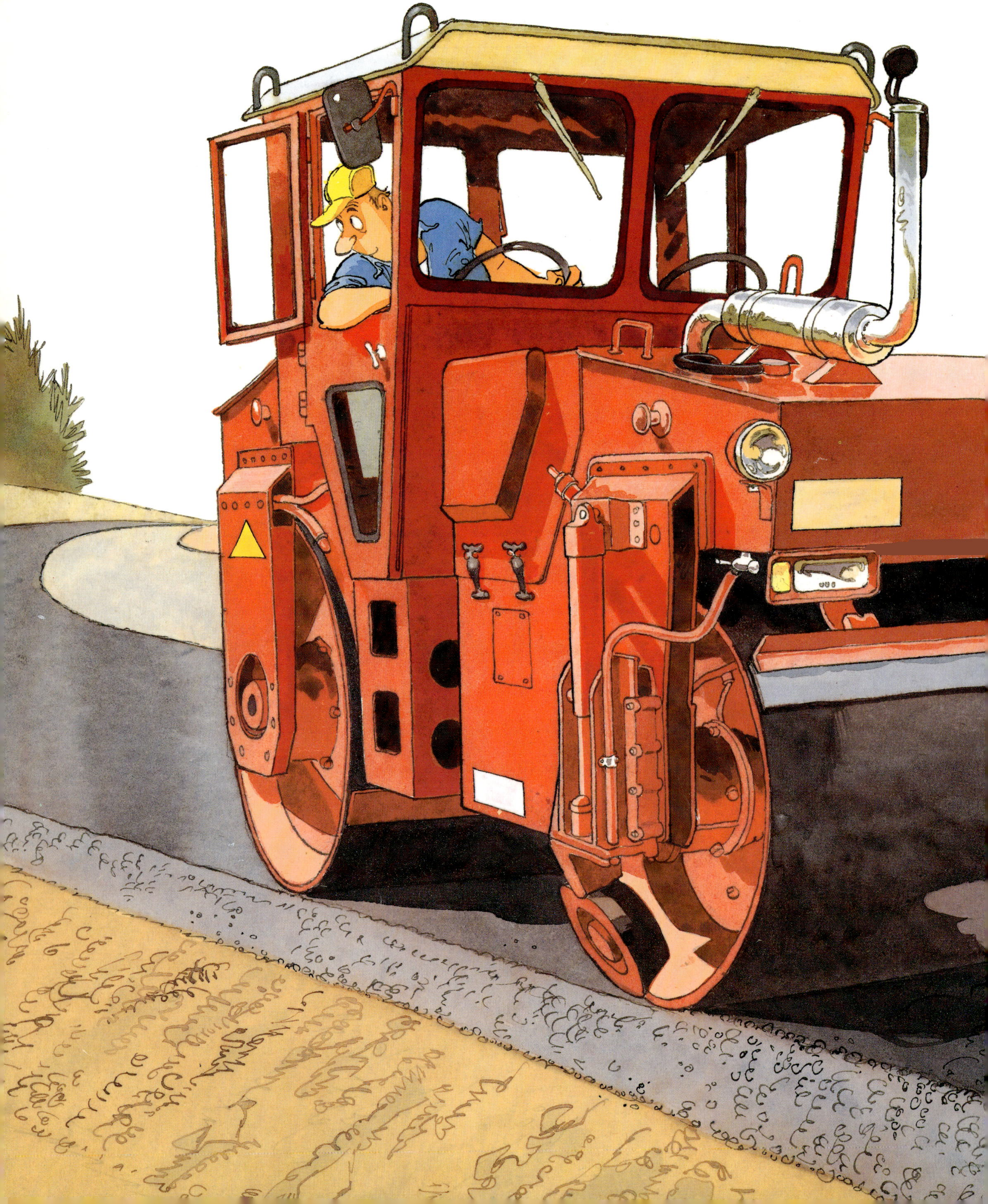

# Road Roller

The road roller follows close behind the paver. Its shuddering roller packs down the hot asphalt.
The asphalt cools to make a tough hard surface for cars and trucks to drive on.

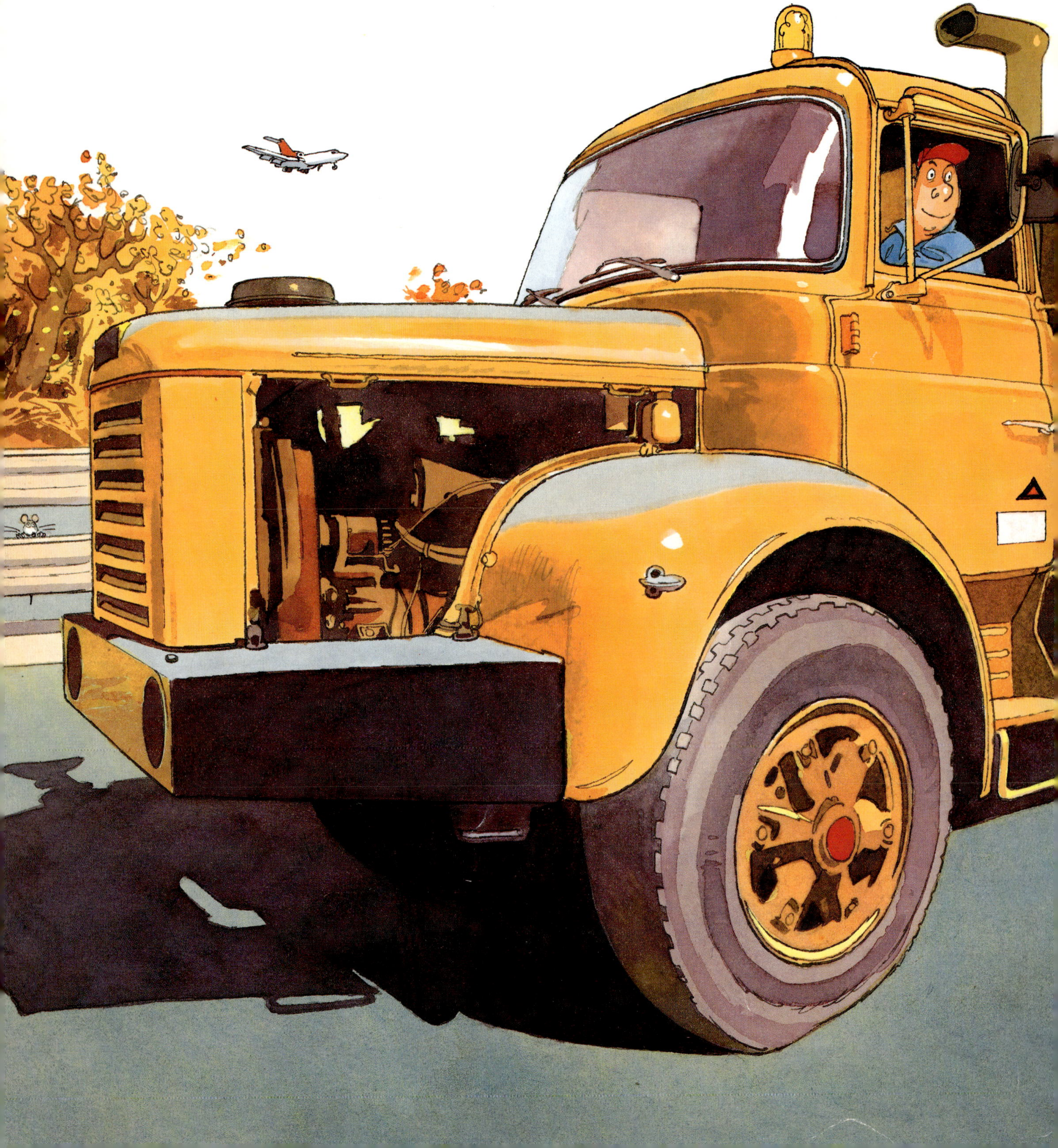

# Roadmarker

This roadmarker sprays white lines onto the road. The lines show drivers where they can go.
Now the new road is finished at last.

Grader

Road Roller

Paver

Roadmarker

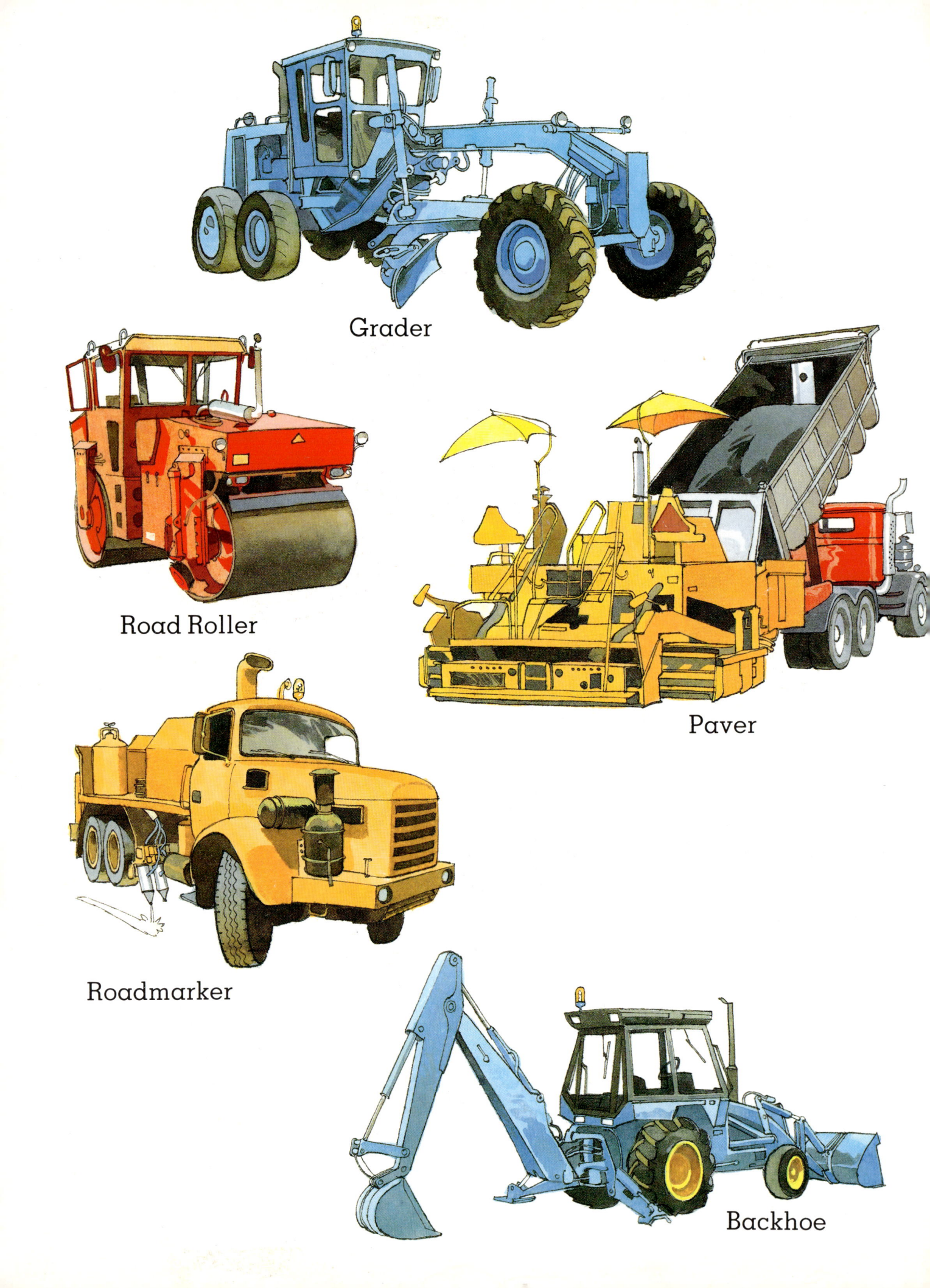

Backhoe